Victoria's Shore Dives

Iñigo Novales Flamarique
Michael Hendry and Ted White

hancock
house

ISBN 0-88839-374-1
Copyright © 1995 Iñigo Novales Flamarique, Michael Hendry and Ted White

Cataloging in Publication Data
Novales Flamarique, Iñigo, 1966–
Victoria's shore dives

Includes index.
ISBN 0-88839-374-1

1. Scuba diving—British Columbia—Victoria Region—
Guidebooks. 2. Victoria Region (B.C.)—Guidebooks.
I. Hendry, Michael, 1970– II. White, Ted, 1971– III. Title.
GV840.S782C36 1995   797.2'3'0971128   C95-910187-X

Edited: Suzanne M. Chin
Production: Suzanne M. Chin
Cover photo: Captain Crunch, a male wolf eel feeding on a red sea urchin.
*James A. Cosgrove, curator of the Royal British Columbia Museum
(Biological Collections).*

Published simultaneously in Canada and the United States by

HANCOCK HOUSE PUBLISHERS LTD.
19313 Zero Avenue, Surrey, B.C. V4P 1M7
(604) 538-1114   Fax (604) 538-2262 ·

HANCOCK HOUSE PUBLISHERS
1431 Harrison Avenue, Blaine, WA 98230-5005
(604) 538-1114   Fax (604) 538-2262

Contents

Acknowledgments

We would like to thank Mr. Joachim Schnorr von Carolsfeld, Mr. Daryl Parkyn and Mr. Paul Lisson for commenting on this work.

I. Why Was This Book Written?

During the past few years at the University of Victoria, our lives embraced the deep abyss of existentialism. We realized none of us were going to make it to the NHL, NBA or NFL and since Quantum Mechanics and General Relativity had already been formulated, the only clear way to proceed was to write a book on dive sites around Victoria. Such clear logic was welcomed by our families and geeky Star Trek-adoring friends who saw their TV sets freed from NHL playoff action. So, with all this love and support around us, we engaged in this most noble of pursuits.

The other, perhaps slightly significant, reason for writing this book is that we love to dive and see the wonders beneath. We cannot explain why, although one of us was born in a bathtub and the other two claim to be Moby Dick in past lives. Whatever, we share an immense interest in marine biology and thought this might be a way of getting others interested.

A dive for us is characterized by the diversity of marine life we encounter and the many fish and invertebrate behaviors we might witness. Although blowing bubbles and doing flips are part of every diver's experience, we have always believed there is more—the unique interaction with animals, the splendor of biological diversity and the fun of just exploring a different world that we hope to convey in writing this book.

This book's intention is not to create an identification guide but to reveal some dives with easy access and provide an introduction to the diversity of marine life in this area. We have therefore included a list of identification guides (see bibliography) for further information. Knowledge of the organisms provide personal satisfaction and conversation after each dive.

As a final note, we would like to make a plea for conservation; the beauty of the ocean lies in its pristine state. We are lucky to live in a region where the waters are still divable. In taking advantage of this opportunity, we must also assume the responsibility of taking care of them, so generations after us can continue to enjoy their splendor. Please abide by all collecting regulations and do not litter. Have some great dives!

II. Map Legend

Road Abbreviations

Adm: Admirals Road
Bay: Bay Street
Bea: Beacon Avenue
Beg: Begbie
Blan: Blanchard
Cad Bay: Cadboro Bay Road
Ch: Chalet Road
Clo: Cloverdale Avenue
Cook: Cook Street
Craig: Craigflower
Doug: Douglas
Esq: Esquimalt
Fr: Fraser Street
Helm: Helmecken
Int: Interurban
Isl Hwy: Island Highway (#1)
Lam: Lampson
Lr: Landsend Road

McK: McKenzie Avenue
Met R: Metchosin Road
MNXR: Mount Newton X Road
Oce B: Ocean Boulevard
Pan: Pandora Street
Pat Hwy: Patricia Bay Highway (#17)
Qua: Quadra Street
Que: Queenswood Drive
Shelb: Shelbourne
RODr: Royal Oak Drive
Sinc: Sinclair Road
Sooke R: Sooke Road
Tat: Tatlow Road
Tel: Telegraph Bay Road
Wal: Wallace Drive
Wilk: Wilkinson Road
WPr: Willis Point Road
Wr: Wain Road
WSr: West Saanich Road

Dive Sites

1. Fisgard Island (Map A)
2. Grafton Road (Map B)
3. Saxe Point (Map B)
4. Flemming Bay Breakwater (Map B)
5. Ogden Point Breakwater (Map C)
6. Baynes Road (Map D)
7. Ten Mile Point (Map D)

8. Spring Bay (Map D)
9. Telegraph Bay (Map D)
10. Cranford Road (Map D)
11. Moses Point (Map E)
12. Deep Cove (Map E)
13. Henderson Point (Map F)
14. Willis Point (Map G)
15. McKenzie Bight (Map G)

SCUBA Dive Shops

DCOS: Deep Cove Ocean Sports
FW: Frank White's
FWs: Frank White's Surf and Scuba
(Sidney location)
OC: Ocean Center
PSD: Peninsula School of Diving (may

be out of business after 1994)
SL: Scuba Land
IDI: International Divers of Victoria
(Family Center) (may be out of business
after 1994)

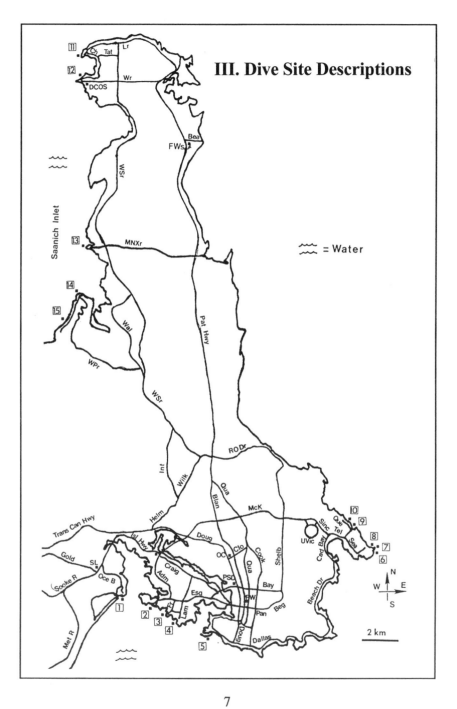

III. Dive Site Descriptions

≈≈ = Water

Saanich Inlet

7

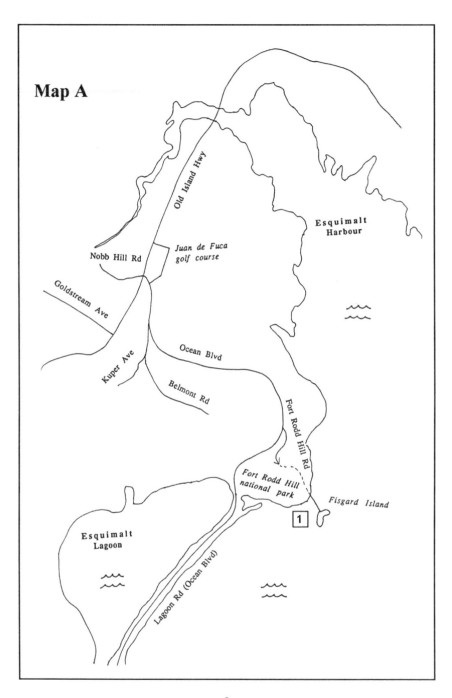

Map A

Old Island Hwy

Esquimalt Harbour

Juan de Fuca golf course

Nobb Hill Rd

Goldstream Ave

Ocean Blvd

Kuper Ave

Belmont Rd

Fort Rodd Hill Rd

Fort Rodd Hill national park

Fisgard Island

1

Esquimalt Lagoon

Lagoon Rd (Ocean Blvd)

1. Fisgard Island

Access to Fisgard Island can sometimes be difficult but if you manage to plan your dive to correspond to Fort Rodd Hill park hours and do not mind a bit of a walk, you will enjoy an excellent shallow dive (there is a $3.00 charge for parking).

The entrance is covered by the rockweed *Fucus distichus* and in the shallow areas, the beautiful small red algae *Iridea* is also present. At about fifteen feet (five meters), the surfgrass *Phyllospadix scouleri* covers some of the rock pockets and the perennial stalk kelp *Pterygophora californica* is common. The soft bottom can be populated by patches of eel grass *(Zostera marina)* and large bottom-covering kelps such as *Laminaria saccharina* and *Agarum fimbriatum.*

Among the invertebrates at this site look for a wide variety of snails including the leafy hornmouth *(Ceratostoma foliatum)* and the blue or costate shell *(Calliostoma ligatum.)* Several species of nudibranchs are usually present including the sea lemons (e.g. the false sea lemon *(Archidoris montereyensis)* and the speckled sea lemon *(Anisodoris nobilis))*, the alabaster or white-lined nudibranch *(Dirona albolineata),* the opalescent *(Hermissenda crassicornis),* the clown *(Triopha catalinae),* and the ringed nudibranch *(Diaulua sandiegensis.)*

Crab species are also abundant and include red rock *(Cancer productus)*, sharp-nosed *(Scyra acutifrons)*, decorator *(Oregonia gracilis)*, dungeness *(Cancer magister)* and kelp crabs *(Pugettia producta)*. The sharp-nosed crab is numerous but can be tricky to spot due to the prominent growths of other invertebrates (e.g. tunicates) on the carapace.

The large tube (or feather duster) worm *(Eudistylia vancouveri)* is common and occasionally covers the rocks along with various species of anemones, making for large beautiful green, purple and red patches. It is fascinating to see these *lawns* of tubeworms quickly withdraw into their tubes upon outside disturbance.

Among the fish species you'll see kelp greenlings *(Hexagrammos decagrammus)*, scalyhead sculpins *(Artedius harringtoni)* and perhaps a ratfish *(Hydrolagus colliei)*.

The rocky perimeter of the island meets a soft bottom (sand and shells) at a maximum of about thirty feet (ten meters).

Map B

Tillicum Rd

Craigflower Rd

Colville Rd

Constance
Cove

Lampson

Admirals Rd

CFB Esquimalt
Dockyard

Esquimalt

Grafton Rd

Lyall

Fraser

2

Saxe Pt. Park

Bewdley Ave

DND Property

Plaskett Pl

Kniver

Munro St

3

4

2. Grafton Road

Grafton Road provides a section of shoreline as interesting as Saxe Point. At the entrance, numerous species of algae compete for space along the almost vertical barnacle-covered walls. Among the algae you will find rockweed, surfgrass and the Turkish towel *(Gigartina papillata.)*

During low tide, *Phyllospadix* and the encrusting coralline *Lithothamnium* can be seen in tidepools covering rocks along with some sponges (e.g. the red sponge, *Ophlithospongia pennata).*

Below the tideline, brown algae, the stalk kelp, *Pterygophora californica* and the bottom-covering blade kelp, *Agarum fimbriatum,* are common. Other kelp usually present in this dive are the sea cabbage *(Hedophyllum sessile),* sea lettuce *(Ulva)* and bull kelp *(Nereocystis luetkeana),* along with a wide variety of anemones including the giant green anemone *(Anthopleura xanthogrammica.)*

Short sections of wall contain caves lined with bright red and yellow sponges and each cave seems to contain its own resident longfin sculpin *(Jordania zanope).* On top of some red sponges, the red nudibranch *(Rostanga pulchra)* may be grazing. Large broken rocks and an abundance of crabs create a haven for the Pacific octopus *(Octopus dofleini).*

All three species of sea urchin (red, *Strongylocentrotus franciscanus,* green, *S. droebachiensis* and purple, *S. purpuratus)* cover many of the rocky areas. Also visible are clusters of plumose anemones *(Metridium senile)* scattered among the rocks.

The gravel and silt bottom along the rocky areas may not seem too appealing, however a short expedition can be worthwhile. On this substrate tadpole sculpins *(Psychrolutes paradoxus)*, *Luidia* mudstars and the buried anemone *(Urticina coriacea)* are sometimes encountered.

Common fish species at this site include lingcod *(Ophiodon elongatus)*, kelp greenlings, striped and pile perch *(Embiotoca lateralis* and *Rhacochilus vacca)* and scalyhead sculpins. Also keep your eyes open for grunt sculpins *(Ramphocottus richardsoni)*.

3. Saxe Point (See map page 12)

Saxe Point is a shallow dive (thirty feet, ten meters or less, unless you love to swim) with an enormous variety of invertebrate life and plenty of room to explore.

From the parking lot entrance, a short swim to the right leads to a gradually-sloping rocky bottom. If you stay close to shore, you will find a section of wall covered with brilliantly-colored anemones, corals, tunicates and sponges.

Among the conspicuous fish here are kelp and whitespotted greenlings *(Hexagrammos stelleri)* and several species of perch. Longfin and scalyhead sculpins are a sure bet and the occasional red Irish lord *(Hemilepidotus hemilepidotus)* and rock greenling *(Hexagrammos lagocephalus)* can be found. Look in the nooks and crannies for mosshead warbonnets *(Chirolophis nugator)* and near bottom covering kelp for Grunt sculpins and manacled sculpins *(Synchirus gilli)*. A few wolf eel pairs *(Anarrhichthys ocellatus)* have also been spotted in the area and surf smelt *(Hypomesus pretiosus pretiosus)* can be seen by disturbing the silt bottom in the bay.

There are various octopus dens scattered around the point. Some can be very conspicuous as they are located under isolated rocks over the silt bottom and exhibit the typical trash heap of remains from past meals (e.g. carapaces, shells).

A fascinating creature often seen at Saxe Point is the lion nudibranch *(Melibe leonina.)* This animal is usually spotted over large kelp or eel grass searching for a crustacean meal. High populations of the northern abalone *(Haliotis kamtschatkana)* are also present, but we stress that these animals *cannot* be collected.

Common snails at this site include the hairy triton *(Fusitriton oregonensis)* the moon snail *(Polinices lewisii)* and *Ceratostoma folliatum.* Saxe point is also a favorite site for the brooding anemone *(Epiactis prolifera)* and tall plumose anemones.

Soft bottom areas are populated by eel grass, on which the hydrozoan jellyfish *(Gonionemus vertens)* is often seen clinging. The sunflower star *(Pycnopodia helianthoides)* can also be seen digging for clams in these areas. Saxe point is characterized by the complex patchwork of algae present. Some of the rocks in shallow areas are completely covered by surf grass, while rich mixtures of eel grass, stalk kelp and bull kelp are present throughout different parts of the site.

On the rocks, branching coralline algaes can form extensive pink mats and, in exposed areas, you may see the feather boa *(Egregia menziesii.)* This algae is distinguished by its thick central strip (about one inch, 2.5 centimeters) bordered by feathery projections and small gas bladders.

Around thirty feet (ten meters) depth straight out from the lookout entrance, a series of warty-looking rock clusters appear. These are built by the reef-building worm *Dodecaceria fewkesi* (look in the holes for this black worm). On various occasions, sea lions *(Zalophus californianus)* have accompanied us while exploring this dive site.

15

4. Flemming Bay Breakwater (See map page 12)

Flemming Bay is a shallow dive with sufficient invertebrate life to keep every diver happy. The breakwater is close to a hundred yards (a hundred meters) long and is made of broken rock that seems to provide ideal habitat for a variety of crab species.

Porcelain crabs *(Petrolisthes eriomerus)* find shelter underneath the rocks and, occasionally, bright orange hermit crabs *(Elassochirus gilli)* living within orange commensal sponges can be found. The breakwater is home to beautifully-colored turtle *(Cryptolithodes sitchensis)*, heart *(Phyllolithodes papillosus)* and kelp crabs. Where the rocks meet the soft bottom and eel grass, look for dungeness and red rock crabs. Attached to the eel grass, look for stalked jellyfish such as the clown *(Halyclistus stejnegeri)* and *Thaumatoscyphus atlanticus.*

Other invertebrate life includes proliferating anemones *(Epiactis prolifera)*, brittle stars *(Ophioplocus esmarkii, Ophiopholis aculeata, Amphipholis squamata)* and several nudibranchs including the white Berthella *(Berthella californica)* and *Melibe leonina.*

Although the abundance of crabs and the rocky substrate would indicate the presence of octopi, we have only seen one octopus at this site so far. Fish to look for are Grunt, longfin and scalyhead sculpins. You will also see kelp greenlings and striped and pile perch.

Examine the cracks and crevices for gunnels (family *Pholidae)*, pricklebacks (family *Stichaeidae)* and northern clingfish *(Gobiesox maeandricus)*. The algae on the rocks consists of small red *(*e.g. *Iridea)* and brown algae, and bottom covering blades like *Agarum fimbriatum*.

Keep an eye out for the sea cabbage and the dead man's fingers *(Halosaccion glandiforme.)* Small patches of bull kelp are also usually present.

Map C

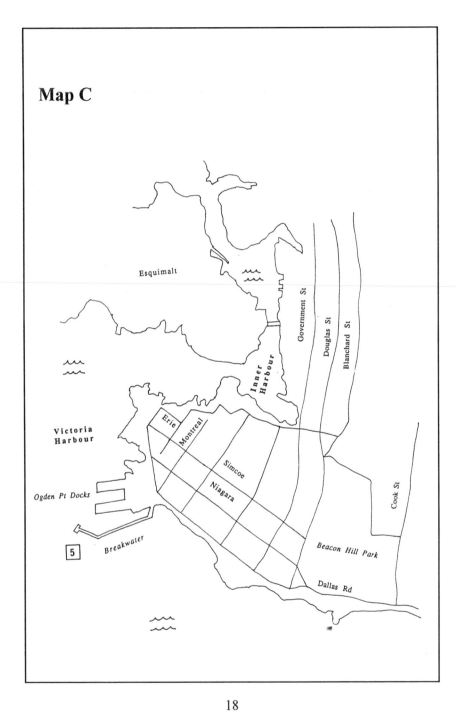

5. Ogden Point Breakwater

The breakwater is the most popular dive site in Victoria and with good reason. A series of stepped boulders gives way to a steep slope of broken rocks that reaches a soft bottom at about eighty feet (twenty-six meters) near its end. This structure makes the breakwater a perfect home for a wide variety of fish and invertebrate life.

Five interpretive plaques with descriptions and pictures of the major fish, invertebrate and plant species inhabiting the breakwater are located at various depths along its length (first one around thirty feet, ten meters). The algae species found at the breakwater are extremely diverse. On the rocks near the beach entrance, large bottom covering algae such as *Agarum* and the sugar kelp *Laminaria saccharina* are prominent.

Over the sandy bottom, sea lettuce and eel grass provide small refuges for schools of perch and juvenile crabs. In shallow waters along the breakwater, small kelps such as the wing kelp *(Alaria marginata)* and the acid kelp *(Desmerestia ligulata)* can be found. This last kelp secretes strong acid when placed in a container (e.g. a bucket), thus its common name.

With increasing depth and wave exposure (i.e. after the first bend) it is mostly the bull kelp that grows in large beds and stalk kelp is present at the edge of these beds. Also, encrusting algae such as *Lithothamnium* are found over the entire boulder and rock range.

The breakwater is a fantastic place for viewing rockfish. You can see copper and quillback, Puget Sound, yellowtail, tiger, black or even, if you are lucky, vermilion or china rockfish *(Sebastes caurinus, S. maliger, S. emphaeus, S. flavidus, S. nigrocinctus, S. melanops, S.miniatus* and *S. nebulosus* in that order). The breakwater is also Victoria's best shore dive for very large lingcod.

Other fishes commonly seen are striped, pile and silver perch *(Hyperprosopon ellipticum)*, tube snouts *(Aulorhynchus flavidus)* and longfin and scaly head sculpins. The invertebrate life is characterized by swimming scallops *(Chlamys hastata)*, plumose anemones and fish-eating anemones *(Urticina piscivora)*.

Creating shadows over a colony of swimming scallops will probably incite some of them to swim in the water column. Their frantic closing and opening of shells is quite humorous to watch. Brittle stars are also numerous and, when the rocks are fairly small, their protruding arms can form what looks like an uncut lawn. Puget Sound king crabs *(Lopholithodes mandtii)* are an occasional treat.

The breakwater is also home to numerous octopi and some wolf eels. Many divers come to feed these animals, luring them with crabs and sea urchins. During one memorable occasion, a large male wolf eel living halfway between the second and third bend came out of its den on our approach. The seven foot (2.3 meter) male circled around us, rubbed against us for a few minutes (as if asking for food), then went back to its hideout. We have never seen this friendly individual again.

During the fall, schools of juvenile herring *(Clupea pallasi)* can be viewed near the bull kelp. If you wait patiently in the surroundings, you'll probably witness quick dashes on the schools by nearby lingcod resting on the rocks, and black rockfish using the kelp as camouflage to approach the schools and claim their prey. The large numbers of fish at the breakwater attract larger predators such as seals *(Phoca vitulina)* and sea lions. These animals are very curious and may swim close to divers for long periods. During night dives, seals have used the beams from our lights to locate black rockfish and prey on them (smart animals!).

Overall, there is plenty of space to dive in this ecological reserve and the fish and invertebrate life varies along the breakwater's length. We recommend you do various dives exploring this great site. When you are wearing all your gear, the end of the breakwater is a long way, but you'll probably find the hike worth the effort.

Map D

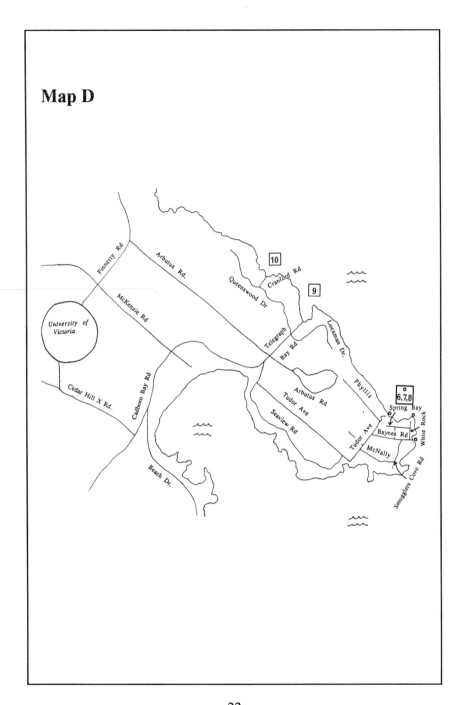

6. Baynes Road

If you have just surfaced from a dive at Ten Mile Point and you let yourself float in the current, chances are you will either drift to this dive site or the San Juan Islands!

After a short swim through a small bay, this dive exhibits a gradually descending rough rocky bottom. In the shallows examine the wide variety of algae including rockweed, sea lettuce, sea cabbage, Turkish towel and the small opalescent red *Iridea*.

Below about thirty feet (ten meters), the bottom becomes a mixture of rock and broken shells which can form drifts in areas of high current. At these depths, stalk kelp can be found as well as the bottom covering *Agarum fimbriatum*.

Clusters of giant barnacles rest on the bottom and large beds of red urchins cover the rocks closer to shore. Mixed with the reds are the occasional purple and green urchins. The bull kelp *(Nereocystis luetkeana)* forms large beds at either side of the bay from which entry is gained.

Some octopus dens are hidden on the rocky perimeter and we have often fed the inhabitants while watching the *Nereocystis* forest wave in the current above us.

Among the common fish are kelp greenlings, copper rockfish and buffalo sculpins *(Enophrys bison)*. In sheltered waters near the shore, examine the surroundings for Pacific spiny lumpsuckers *(Eumicrotremus orbis)*.

Also try spotting smooth alligator fish *(Anoplagonus inermis)* hidden among the rocks and kelp.

7. Ten Mile Point (See map page 22)

Ten Mile Point is an excellent dive with the richness of life that comes with rocky substrates and high currents (so watch those tide tables and plan accordingly!). It's sometimes difficult to see the rocks beneath the filter feeders!

Giant barnacles *(Balanus nubilus)*, creeping sea cucumbers *(Psolus chitinoides)*, compound or solitary seasquirts or tunicates *(Ascidians*, e.g. the sea blubber, *Cystodytes lobatus)*, northern abalone and a variety of sponges create a brilliantly colored carpet. Among these, probably the most abundant animals are the large clumps of purple and orange colonial ascidians.

Ten Mile Point is a great site for viewing stony *(coral-like)* bryozoans such as northern and southern staghorns (genus *Heteropora)*, the lacy bryozoan *(Phidolopora labiata),* California hydrocoral and lacy corals. Nudibranchs are also numerous and include the colored dendronotid *(Dendronotus diversicolor)*, Cockerell's dorid *(Laila cockerelli)* and the clown *(Triopha catalinae)* commonly observed feeding on numerous hydroids.

Octopus dens are also a common sight and the animals are sometimes seen outside their hideouts, especially during evening dives.

From the entrance to the dive, there is a short, steeply sloped rocky section, then a wall that drops to approximately eighty feet (twenty-six meters). The steeply sloped rocky region is usually covered with the table top tunicate *(Chelyosoma productum)* and many types of algae such as *Desmerestia, Agarum, Laminaria* and *Pterygophora.* Bull kelp starts forming a small bed as the point toward Baynes Road is approached. The fish life is as diverse as the invertebrate life; copper and quillback rockfish, kelp greenlings, scalyhead and longfin sculpins are always present.

This site is also the home of the great cabezon (Spanish for 'fat head', *Scorpaenichthys marmoratus)*, a big fish with an amazing gape that is extremely gentle (you can sometimes pick one up!). Look also for decorated warbonnets *(Chirolophis decoratus)* and red Irish lords hidden among the rocks and kelp. Sailfin sculpins *(Nautichthys oculofasciatus)* hide in the rocks during the day, but are a common sight in the open at night. Examine the barnacles near the surface for the presence of rockheads as well *(Bothragonus swani).*

Ten Mile Point and the surrounding coastline (Baynes Road, Spring Bay dives) is a sanctuary or ecological reserve. You *cannot* collect specimens nor spear fish.

Angling from shore is nonetheless allowed, so this site and Ogden Point breakwater are great spots for collecting fishing lures entangled in the kelp!

8. Spring Bay (See map page 22)

Spring Bay can be a high-current dive and the invertebrate life present reflects this. A steep, rocky slope begins near the entrance and drops to below seventy feet (twenty-three meters).

The algae is a mixture similar to that at Ten Mile Point, but the *Agarum* cover is greater at this site due to the lack of cliffs. *Pterygophora* covers some rock patches and bull kelp is located at the right side of the bay. Large clumps of giant barnacles provide shelter from the current for small fish and swimming invertebrates. Attached to the barnacles are the spiny-headed tunicate *(Boltenia villosa)* and the warty tunicate *(Pyura haustor.)* Inside and between barnacles, look for the small crab *(Cancer oregonensis.)* Some of these fellows have entered empty barnacle casings while juveniles and have later outgrown the entrance.

Inspect the surroundings also for the small red nudibranch *(Rostanga pulchra)* as well as *Triopha catalinae, Dirona albolineata* and *Laila cockerelli.* At about fifty to sixty feet (sixteen to twenty meters) on the muddy bottom lie colonies of the horse mussel *Modiolus rectus*, partly immersed in the sand. Swimming scallops are also found at these depths.

Common fish in this site include cabezons, buffalo sculpins, copper rockfish and kelp greenlings. You may also see the odd Pacific spiny lumpsucker, or a ratfish in the evening. Schools of tubesnouts are sometimes present. Spend some time looking throughout the clumps of barnacles for Grunt sculpins, decorated warbonnets, gunnels and high cockscombs *(Anoplarchus purpurescens)*.

9. Telegraph Bay (See map page 22)

This is a shallow dive with small currents and easy access, but there is plenty to see. As such, it is a perfect site for beginners just getting used to the underwater environment. Experienced divers will also enjoy this dive, but it will require some swimming to reach even moderate depths (i.e. thirty feet, ten meters).

The bay has a soft muddy bottom interspersed with patches of eel grass and steeply sloped rocky sides. The bottom near the beach entrance experiences little current or wave action and is often covered by kelp (the sea lettuce *Ulva* and the large *Agarum),* and a thin layer of sediment. Toward the mouth of the bay however, the substrate becomes progressively more interesting (for those of us who do not specialize in muddy bottoms...).

Here, broken rocks and a good supply of red rock crabs make ideal octopus habitat. Many decorator-type crabs, such as the true decorator *(Oregonia gracilis)*, the sharp-nosed crab and *Pugettia gracilis* are commonly found. Red urchins dot the rocks and cucumbers such as the California sea cucumber *(Parastichopus californicus)* and the orange sea cucumber *(Cucumaria miniata)* are very common. Small copper rockfish shelter in crevices and longfin sculpins can also be seen, sometimes hanging upside down!

Encountering the little mouse-like Grunt sculpin and following its walking movements from crevice to crevice under the kelp is always a treat. Also, look carefully for gunnels and high cockscombs as they sneak between crevices and only their small heads protrude to observe the surrounding activity. The algae found on the rocky surfaces vary with exposure to current and depth (a phenomenon generally known as *zonation*).

Near the tideline, at the entrance, rockweed is most prominent. At shallow depths, brown and red algae (such as the Turkish towel) cover the rocks. Near the rocky slope, in deeper areas of the bay, bull kelp starts making its presence. Here, covering the rocks, is the encrusting red algae that looks like pink paint: *Lithothamnium*.

During the early spring and fall the deeper portions of the bay are home to big zooplankton and schools of sandlance *(Ammodytes hexapterus)* that feed on them. At this time one may see large jellyfish cruising through the water in search of unexpected prey.

Before you surface from this dive, swim again over the mud bottom and try to spot buried crabs, anemones, clams and other animals associated with a soft substrate.

10. Cranford Road (See map page 22)

This is a shallow dive (less than forty-five feet, fifteen meters deep) offering many surprises to those willing to search among the kelp. The rocks that constitute the beach entrance rapidly change to a kelp blade-covered bottom (mostly *Agarum*).

At about fifteen feet (five meters) depth, the substrate shifts to a silt bottom with scattered empty clam shells and crab carapaces. Plant life here is dominated by *Agarum* with some eel grass. Among the *Agarum* mat, California sea cucumbers, decorator and kelp crabs, sea stars (e.g. the blood star, *(Henricia leviuscula)* and *Pycnopodia helianthoides*), nudibranchs like *Dirona albolineata* and *Triopha catalinae,* and gumboot chitons *(Cryptochiton stelleri)* are easily located. There are also plenty of shrimp among the kelp and rocky substrates, and you may spot a helmet crab *(Telmessus cheiragonus)*.

Fish such as the Grunt sculpin, gunnels, copper rockfish, kelp greenlings and schools of tubesnouts, solitary pipefish *(Syngnathus griseolineatus)* and juvenile herring are usually present. Other, less common, are manacled sculpins and pacific spiny lumpsuckers.

The rock sides bordering the beach and the perimeter of the bay are covered by cup coral *(Balanophyllia elegans)*, sponges and encrusting algae. These slopes offer a combination of crevice and kelp habitat exploited by red and green urchins, sea stars, sea cucumbers, anemones and juvenile fish. Such habitat is also found at the limits of the bay (about thirty-five feet, twelve meters depth) where current can be noticeable.

Overall, this dive resembles Telegraph Bay but with more current.

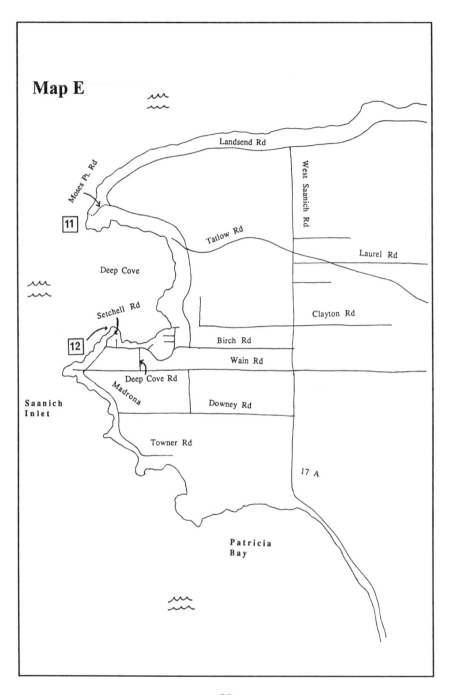

Map E

Landsend Rd

Moses Pt. Rd

West Saanich Rd

11

Tatlow Rd

Laurel Rd

Deep Cove

Clayton Rd

Setchell Rd

12

Birch Rd

Wain Rd

Deep Cove Rd

Madrona

Saanich Inlet

Downey Rd

Towner Rd

17 A

Patricia Bay

11. Moses Point

Well, this is a mud bottom dive, but a good one!

One immediately noticeable characteristic is the large number of red rock crabs and shrimp (e.g. the coonstripe shrimp, *Pandalus danae*). Nudibranchs like *Dirona albolineata* and *Triopha catalinae* are also abundant. The bottom is sprinkled with the buried anemone *(Urticina coriacea.)* Look closely among the tentacles for small commensal shrimp.

Patches of small rocks contain orange sea cucumbers and different species of perch swimming above. Look also in old jars and bottles for the presence of snailfish (*Liparis* species). The algae at this site include rockweed and sea lettuce on the rocks closer to the surface and kelp blades *(Agarum* and *Laminaria)* over the bottom (surprise, surprise...).

Digging the soft bottom may produce some unexpected fish such as surf smelt and buried sandlance. The slope of the bottom is very gradual but divers with the desire to swim may get deeper than sixty feet (twenty meters).

You may try diving to the left of the entry as we have been told it holds the potential for deeper diving.

12. Deep Cove (See map page 32)

Shore access at Deep Cove is possible in a couple of places. One popular dive is a sunken barge a short swim from the dock off Madrona Drive. Another good dive can also be enjoyed from the southwest side of the cove.

The cove's moderately-sloped bottom is a patchwork of soft sediment and rock outcroppings. The algae cover is dominated by *Agarum* blades but *Sargassum* is also present.

The fish and invertebrate life includes a bit of everything. Look for copper rockfish, blackeye gobies *(Coryphopterus nicholsi)*, northern ronquils *(Ronquilus jordani)*, buffalo and longfin sculpins. We have also enjoyed a few good encounters with wolf eels and octopi.

Some soft-bottomed areas contain tube-dwelling anemones and their nemesis, the giant nudibranch *(Dendronotus iris.)* Other nudibranchs present are *Dirona abolineata* and *Triopha catalinae*. Cucumbers range from *Parastichopus californicus* to the small white sea cucumber *(Eupenctacta quinquesemita.)* Large masses of the ribbed whelk snail *(Nucella emarginata)* can be seen laying eggs in the winter and early spring.

An interesting anecdote from this site is the time we saw a sea butterfly *(Gastropteron pacificum),* a rarely encountered animal related to snails and nudibranchs. The swimming motion is achieved by flapping two parapodia (wing equivalents), making the animal look like an underwater butterfly. When disturbed, the sea butterfly folds its wings and settles on the muddy bottom next to rocks, becoming almost invisible. This episode made us wonder how many times we had passed beautiful animals like this one without perceiving them...

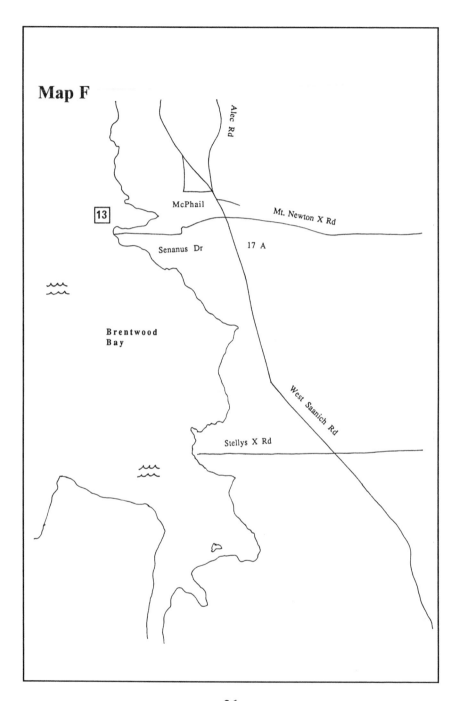

Map F

Alec Rd

McPhail

13

Mt. Newton X Rd

Senanus Dr

17 A

Brentwood
Bay

West Saanich Rd

Stellys X Rd

36

13. Henderson Point

Henderson Point provides a mixture of soft- and rock-bottom diving. Shallow areas are characterized by rockweed, sea lettuce and *Sargassum* below the tide line. Deeper locations are populated by carpets of *Agarum* and some *Laminaria*.

Extensive rocky reefs are dotted with large plumose anemones. Schools of pile and striped perch swim over the shallower portions of the reefs which drop off into steep rocky slopes and cliffs conferring to this site great potential for spectacular underwater scenery, if the visibility is good.

Look for painted and white-spotted greenlings, lingcod and copper and quillback rockfish. Blackeye gobies are also a common sight. Soft-bottom areas have tube-dwelling anemones *(Pachycerianthus fimbriatus)* and the starfish, *Solaster dawsoni*; you may find the latter attacking another starfish.

One of the fun pastimes at this dive site is watching painted greenling gulp small shrimp.

Map G

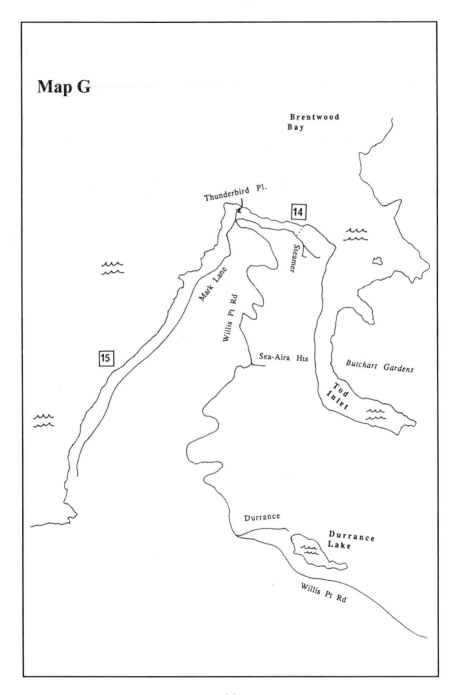

Brentwood Bay

Thunderbird Pl.

14

Steamer

Mark Lane

Willis Pt Rd

15

Sea-Aira Hts

Butchart Gardens

Tod Inlet

Durrance

Durrance Lake

Willis Pt Rd

14. Willis Point

This is one dive site that *must* be experienced. The entrance is covered with rockweed and sea lettuce, and *Sargassum* can also be seen in the shallows.

With increasing depth, blade kelps *(Agarum* and *Laminaria)* cover the ocean floor. These two algae can form a very thick mat, providing excellent refuge for a wide variety of animals. Within a hundred feet (thirty-three meters) of the entrance, a series of cliffs begin that drop to depths well below 150 feet (fifty meters). If the visibility is good, the views can be spectacular. If not, one may still enjoy the experience of floating over what looks like a bottomless abyss.

Sometimes, at this and other inlet dives, there is a phytoplankton layer a few meters thick at the surface. Beneath this layer visibility improves once again but the light levels are drastically reduced even at moderate depths (forty to fifty feet, thirteen to sixteen meters). As a result, it is a good idea to carry a light (actually, you should *always* carry a light!).

In deeper sections of the wall (seventy-five feet or more, twenty-five meters), boot sponges *(Rhabdocalyptus dawsoni)* are abundant along with galatheid crabs (squat lobsters, *Munida quadrispina)* that inhabit the cracks and crevices. A couple of large octopus dens are also easily accessible.

This dive and others in Saanich Inlet are great places to look for the large lion's mane scyphozoan *(Cyanea capillata),* a jellyfish. Be careful not to touch them with exposed skin as these animals have a mild sting to which some people are highly allergic.

Among the common fish species are the copper and quillback rockfish and blackeye goby. In shallower water, look for the hairy lithode crab *(Haplogaster mortansii)*, Grunt sculpins and pile and striped perch.

Careful inspections of cracks in the wall may reveal a decorated warbonnet as well. You may also see a northern spearnose poacher *(Agonopsis vulsa)* over soft substrate usually between forty and seventy feet (thirteen to twenty-three meters).

Lucky divers have spotted the fabled six gill shark *(Hexanchus griseus)* at this location but most people only get to see a dogfish *(Squalus acanthias)* if any elasmobranch at all.

15. Mckenzie Bight (See map page 38)

The bight is Victoria's best chance for great visibility. It is seldom rough and currents are weak. There is more than a quarter of a mile of water to explore, with various access locations.

In shallow areas, the bottom consists of patches of soft substrate mixed with large rock outcroppings. As you get deeper, the slope increases and in most places a series of cliffs start between seventy and a hundred feet (twenty-three to thirty-three meters).

Rockweed is present in great numbers at the tideline. Other algae are the Turkish towel and *Sargassum*. In the shallows, brown and red algae are common on the rocks, while large growths of the blade kelp *Agarum* cover most of the ocean floor.

Among the common invertebrates are boot sponges and tube-dwelling anemones *(Pachycerianthus fimbriatus)* extending over large areas of soft bottom. You can also see several cloud sponges *(Aphrocallistes vastus)* interspersed among the reefs. Look for the giant nudibranch *(Dendronotus iris)* among the tube-dwelling anemones.

Also over the soft bottom is a healthy population of the sunflower star *(Pycnopodia helianthoides)*, its reign of terror over the invertebrate world only temporarily interrupted by the presence of the morning star *(Solaster dawsoni)*.

In the summer, the light bulb tunicate *(Clavelina huntsmani)* and the tube worm *(Phylochaetopterus prolifica)* are found in great numbers among the red algal mat at twenty to thirty feet (six to ten meters). Other invertebrates commonly found at this site are the hairy 'tennis ball' tunicate *(Halocynthia igaboja)* and the swimming anemone *(Stomphia coccinia)* (at seventy feet [twenty-three meters] and deeper).

At shallow depths you will see schools of perch and, near the rocks, copper rockfish feeding on small crustaceans. Some individuals may even be in the process of giving birth.

Carry a red rock crab if you find one and keep an eye out for octopus and wolf eel dens (in 1994, at least one wolf eel pair and one octopus inhabited each of the four major reefs making up this dive site). The nooks and crannies of the shallow parts of the reefs are home to various species of shrimp such as *Pandalus danae*. With increasing depth, these are replaced by squat lobsters.

Near the bottom, quillback and copper rockfish hover over rocks, patrolling their territories. Other common fish at this site are lingcod, blackeye gobies and ronquils.

You may also see a northern spearnose poacher or even some shark species such as the six gill shark, salmon shark *(Lamna ditropis)* or basking shark *(Cetorhinus maximus)* if you are *really* lucky!

IV. Popular Fish (Adults)

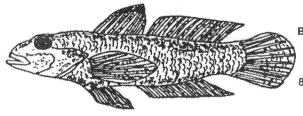

Blackeye goby *(Coryphopterus nicholsi)*. Orange-yellow color with prominent black around eye. Sizes: 8-15 centimeters.

Black rockfish *(Sebastes melanops)*. Color: Black-grayish with some lighter spots and white belly. Sizes: 30-60 centimeters.

Cabezon *(Scorpaenichthys marmoratus)*. Color: mottled marble-brown. Sizes: 60-95 centimeters.

Copper rockfish *(Sebastes caurinus)*. Variable from dull brown to copper pink with mixtures of yellow, copper or even red patches. Sizes: 30-55 centimeters.

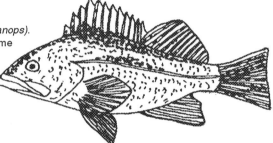

Decorated warbonnet *(Chirolophis decoratus).* Color: pale pinkish-brown with white markings. Sizes: 20-45 centimeters.

Rockweed gunnel *(Xererpes fucorum).* Color: bright green to red with some darker spots. Sizes: 14-20 centimeters.

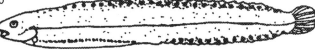

Grunt sculpin *(Rhamphocottus richardsoni).* Variable, often green-brownish patches over a pinkish-white background. Sizes: 5-10 centimeters.

Herring *(Clupea pallasi).* Color: silver gray with some green. Sizes: 20-30 centimeters.

43

High cockscomb *(Anoplarchus purpurescens)*. Color: variable, light gray to brown and black with overtones of blue and red. Sizes: 10-20 centimeters.

Kelp greenling *(Hexagrammos decagrammus)*. Females yellowish-brown to gray with reddish-brown spots, males gray-brown with prominent blue spots surrounded by rings of red near the head. Yellowish fins. Sizes: 30-60 centimeters.

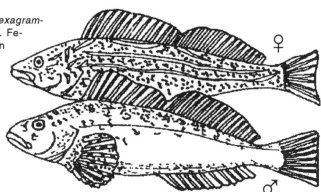

Mosshead warbonnet *(Chirolophis nugator)*. Color: red-pinkish with dark eyespots along dorsal fin. Sizes: 8-15 centimeters.

Lingcod *(Ophiodon elongatus)*. Brown-gray to silver-gray with dark spots throughout most of the body. Sizes: 80-150 centimeters.

44

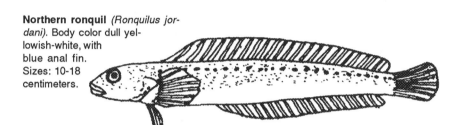

Marbled snailfish *(Liparis dennyi).* Color variable, but usually white and black longitudinal patterns across body. Sizes: 20-30 centimeters.

Northern ronquil *(Ronquilus jordani).* Body color dull yellowish-white, with blue anal fin. Sizes: 10-18 centimeters.

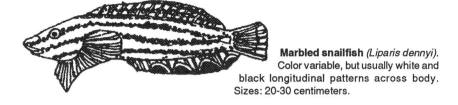

Northern spearnose poacher *(Agonopsis emmelane).* Coloration brownish to grayish. Sizes: 14-20 centimeters.

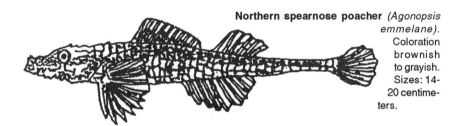

Painted greenling *(Oxylebius pictus).* Color: red bands on a whitish background. Sizes: 15-25 centimeters.

45

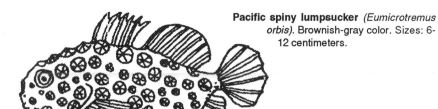

Pacific spiny lumpsucker *(Eumicrotremus orbis)*. Brownish-gray color. Sizes: 6-12 centimeters.

Pile perch *(Rhacochilus vacca)*. Body color bright silver with yellowish-white fins. Sizes: 25-45 centimeters.

Quillback rockfish *(Sebastes maliger)*. Brown color with lighter areas on the anterior part. Sizes: 30-60 centimeters.

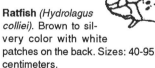

Ratfish *(Hydrolagus colliei)*. Brown to silvery color with white patches on the back. Sizes: 40-95 centimeters.

46

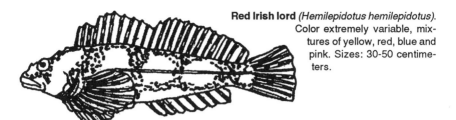

Red Irish lord *(Hemilepidotus hemilepidotus)*. Color extremely variable, mixtures of yellow, red, blue and pink. Sizes: 30-50 centimeters.

Rockhead *(Bathragonus swani)*. Color: variable, from bright red to dark brown. Sizes: 5-9 centimeters.

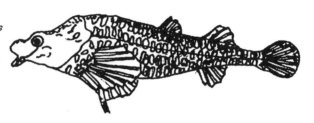

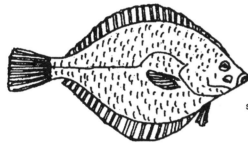

Rock sole *(Lepidopsetta bilineata)*. Brownish body color with small dark patches. Sizes: 30-60 centimeters. This and other left-eye flounders are sometimes found camouflaged on sandy bottoms.

Scalyhead sculpin *(Artedius harringtoni)*. Color variable but typically red. Sizes: 6-10 centimeters.

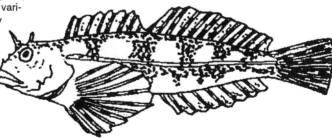

Surf smelt *(Hypomesus pretiosus pretiosus)*. Color: silver with olive-green on the back. Sizes: 20-30 centimeters.

Striped seaperch *(Embiotoca lateralis)*. Brownish-copper color with silvery horizontal lines and greenish belly. Sizes: 20-35 centimeters.

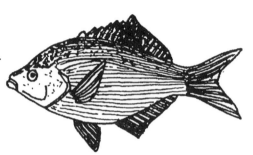

Tiger rockfish *(Sebastes nigrocinctus)*. Color: five or six vertical dark red bands over a pinkish-whitish background. Sizes: 30-60 centimeters.

Tube-snout *(Aulorhynchus flavidus)*. Color: silvery gray. Sizes: 10-20 centimeters.

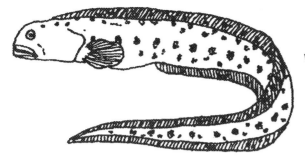

Wolf eel *(Anarrhichthys ocellatus).* Color: white to silvery blue with dark spots surrounded by white halos. Sizes: 1-2.5 meters.

Yellowtail rockfish *(Sebastes flavidus).* Green-brownish coloration and pale yellow fins and tail. Sizes: 40-65 centimeters.

49

V. Popular Invertebrates (Adults)

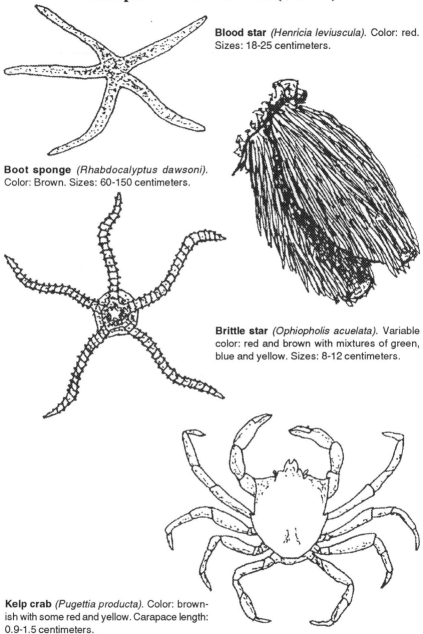

Blood star *(Henricia leviuscula)*. Color: red. Sizes: 18-25 centimeters.

Boot sponge *(Rhabdocalyptus dawsoni)*. Color: Brown. Sizes: 60-150 centimeters.

Brittle star *(Ophiopholis acuelata)*. Variable color: red and brown with mixtures of green, blue and yellow. Sizes: 8-12 centimeters.

Kelp crab *(Pugettia producta)*. Color: brownish with some red and yellow. Carapace length: 0.9-1.5 centimeters.

California sea cucumber *(Parastichopus californicus)*. Color: variable, usually dark reddish-brown. Sizes: 30-50 centimeters.

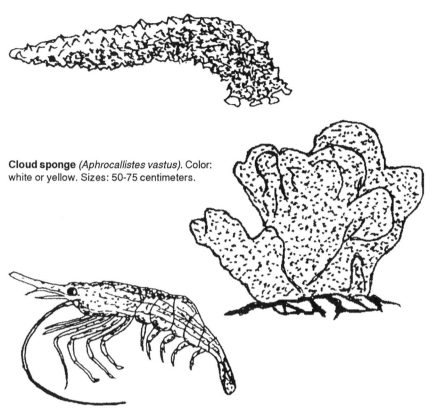

Cloud sponge *(Aphrocallistes vastus)*. Color: white or yellow. Sizes: 50-75 centimeters.

Coonstripe shrimp *(Pandalus danae)*. Color: Translucent with red, brown and black marks. Size: 9-14 centimeters.

Creeping cucumber *(Psolus chitonoides)*. Color: Red-brown and orange. Sizes: 9-12 centimeters.

51

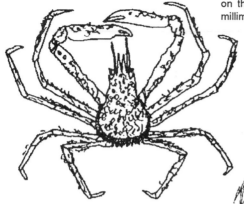

Decorator crab *(Oregonia gracilis)*. Color: variable, brown and red; other colors dependent on dead and living plants and animals on the carapace. Carapace length: 45-65 millimeters.

Feather duster tube worm *(Eudistylia vancouveri)*. Brown and green feather tentacles in brownish tube. Sizes: 30-45 centimeters.

Fish eating anemone *(Urticina piscivora)*. Color: olive-yellow. Sizes: 15-30 centimeters.

Giant barnacle *(Balanus nubilus)*. Red-yellow lips giving rise to brown-black tentacles inside a white-brownish casing. Sizes: 7-10 centimeters.

Giant nudibranch *(Dendronotus iris)*. Color: variable, gray to gray-brown to orange-red. Sizes: 8-25 centimeters.

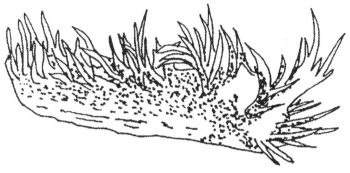

Gumboot chiton *(Cryptochiton stelleri)*. Color: red to brown. Sizes: 25-35 centimeters.

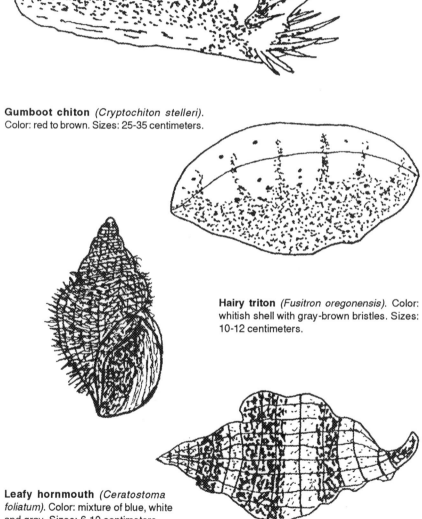

Hairy triton *(Fusitron oregonensis)*. Color: whitish shell with gray-brown bristles. Sizes: 10-12 centimeters.

Leafy hornmouth *(Ceratostoma foliatum)*. Color: mixture of blue, white and gray. Sizes: 6-10 centimeters.

53

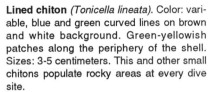

Lined chiton *(Tonicella lineata)*. Color: variable, blue and green curved lines on brown and white background. Green-yellowish patches along the periphery of the shell. Sizes: 3-5 centimeters. This and other small chitons populate rocky areas at every dive site.

Lions-mane scyphozoan *(Cyanea capillata)*. Transparent with yellow-reddish tentacles. Sizes: bell up to 50 centimeters, tentacles up to three meters.

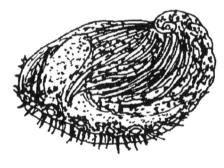

Northern abalone *(Haliotis kamtschatkana)*. Color: red-brownish with some gray and green mixtures. Sizes: 12-18 centimeters.

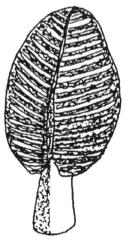

Orange sea pen *(Ptilosarcus gurneyi)*. Color: orange-yellowish. Sizes: 30-100 centimeters. Very rarely seen, sometimes in deep waters (80 feet [26 meters]) in Saanich Inlet.

54

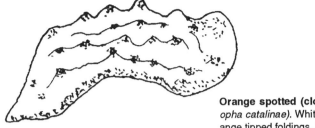

Orange spotted (clown) nudibranch *(Triopha catalinae)*. White colored body with orange tipped foldings. Sizes: 5-7 centimeters.

Pacific giant octopus *(Octopus dofleini)*. Color: changed at will, sometimes red-brown. Sizes: 1-3.5 meters. Maximum 7 meters.

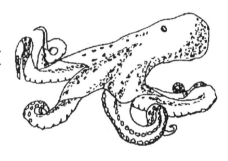

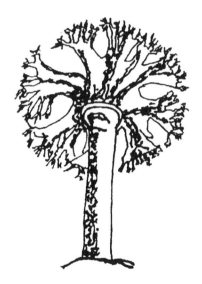

Plumose anemone *(Metridium senile)*. Color: white or orange. Sizes: 30-90 centimeters (in height).

Warty tunicate *(Pyura haustor)*. Color: orange-brown with red siphons. Sizes: 3-6 centimeters.

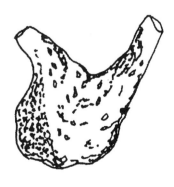

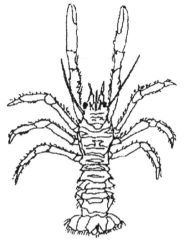

Squat lobster *(Munida quadrispina)*. Color: brown-red. Sizes: 2-6.5 centimeters.

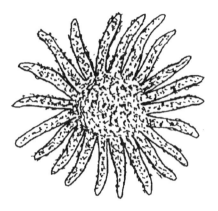

Sunflower star *(Pycnopodia helianthoides)*. Color: variable orange, purple or brown-gray. Sizes: 50-100 centimeters.

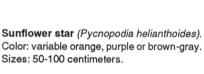

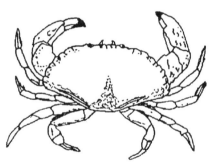

Red rock crab *(Cancer productus)*. Red carapace with black tipped claws. Carapace length: 15-20 centimeters.

Swimming scallop *(Chlamys hastata)*. Orange to brown orange in color. Sizes: 6-10 centimeters.

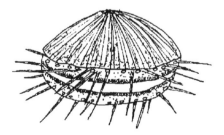

56

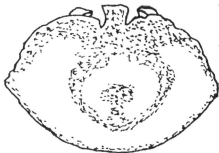

Turtle or umbrella crab *(Cryptolithodes sitchensis).* Color: highly variable, mixtures of orange, brown, pink, red, gray, purple and white. Carapace length: 7-9 centimeters.

Sea urchin (genus *Strongylocentrotus).* Color: three species, green, purple or red. Sizes: Green and purple 6-9 centimeters, red 10-15 centimeters. Spines of red are about 8 centimeters long, double of those from the other two species.

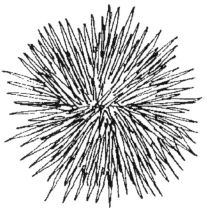

VI. Important Telephone Numbers

Decompression Chambers

Vancouver General Hospital:
876-3211
Fleet Diving Unit:
380-2379
CAN Dive Diving Services:
988-3029

Others

Rescue Coordination Center,
Marine and Aircraft Stress:
1-800-567-5111

All types of emergencies:

911

VII. Major SCUBA Shops

Deep Cove Ocean Sports
10992 Madrona Drive
RR#1, Sidney, BC
Tel: 656-0060

Frank White's (Surf and Scuba)
2537 Beacon Street
Sidney, BC
Tel: 656-9202

Frank White's
1855 Blanshard Street
Victoria, BC
Tel: 385-4713

Ocean Center
800 Cloverdale Avenue
Victoria, BC
Tel: 475-2202

Peninsula School of Diving (and Underwater Sports)
2519 Douglas Street
Victoria, BC
Tel: 386-3483

VIII. Bibliography

Behrens, D.W. 1980. *Pacific Coast Nudibranchs.* Sea Challengers Publishers.

Carefoot, T. 1977. *Pacific Seashores, a Guide to Intertidal Ecology.* J. J. Douglas Ltd.

Gotshall, D. W. and Laurent, L. L. 1979. *Pacific Coast Subtidal Marine Invertebrates.* Sea Challengers Publishers.

Harbo, R. M. 1984. *Tidepool and Reef: Marinelife Guide to the Pacific Northwest.* Hancock House Publishers Ltd.

Harbo, R. M. 1988. *Guide to the Western Seashore.* Hancock House Publishers Ltd.

Hart, J. F. L. 1982. *Crabs and Their Relatives of British Columbia.* British Columbia Provincial Museum Publishers.

Hart, J. L. 1974. *Pacific Fishes of Canada.* Ottawa, Fisheries Research Board of Canada, bulletin 180.

Kozloff, E. N. 1987. *Marine Invertebrates of the Pacific Northwest.* University of Washington Press.

Kozloff, E. N. 1983. *Seashore Life of the Northern Pacific Coast.* Douglas and McIntyre Publishers.

Lamb, A. and Edgell, P. 1986. *Coastal Fishes of the Pacific Northwest.* Harbour Publishing.

Love, R. M. 1991. *Probably More Than You Want to Know About the Fishes of the Pacific Coast.* Really Big Press Publishers Company.

Nybakken, J. W. 1982. *Marine Biology, an Ecological Approach.* Harper and Row Publishers.

IX. List of Organisms Mentioned

Scientific name: *Common name*   **Page**

61

WESTERN GUIDES

**Alpine
Wildflowers**
J. E. (Ted) Underhill
ISBN 0-88839-975-8
5½ x 8½ SC   6.95

**Coastal Lowland
Wildflowers**
J. E. (Ted) Underhill
ISBN 0-88839-973-1
5½ X 8½ SC   6.95

**Sagebrush
Wildflowers**
J. E. (Ted) Underhill
ISBN 0-88839-171-4
5½ x 8 ½ SC   6.95

**Upland Field & Forest
Wildflowers**
J. E. (Ted) Underhill
ISBN 0-88839-174-9
5½ x 8½ SC   6.95

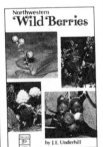

**Northwestern
Wild Berries**
J. E. (Ted) Underhill
ISBN 0-88839-027-0
5½ x 8½ SC   8.95

Wild Harvest
Edible Plants of the Pacific Northwest
Terry Domico
ISBN 0-88839-022-X
5½ x 8½ SC   7.95

**Rocks & Minerals
of the Northwest**
Stan & Chris Leaming
ISBN 0-88839-053-X
5½ x 8½ SC   4.95

**Western
Mushrooms**
J. E. (Ted) Underhill
ISBN 0-88839-031-9
5 ½ x 8½ SC   4.95

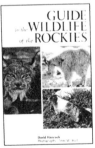

**Wildlife
of the Rockies**
David Hancock
ISBN 0-919654-33-9
5½ x 8½ SC   3.50

Guide to the
Western Seashore
Rick M. Harbo
ISBN 0-88839-201-X
5 1/2 x 8 1/2, SC   5.95

**Tidepool
& Reef**
Rick M. Harbo
ISBN 0-88839-039-4
5 1/2 x 8 1/2, SC   6.95

**The Edible
Seashore**
Rick M. Harbo
ISBN 0-88839-199-4
5½ X 8½ SC   **$5.95**